Hannibal

Translated by
Aubrey de Sélincourt

PENGUIN BOOKS

PENGUIN CLASSICS

UK | USA | Canada | Ireland | Australia
India | New Zealand | South Africa

Penguin Classics is part of the Penguin Random House group of companies
whose addresses can be found at global.penguinrandomhouse.com.

This selection first published in Penguin Classics 2016
003

Set in 9/12.4 pt Baskerville 10 Pro
Typeset by Jouve (UK), Milton Keynes
Printed and bound in Great Britain by Clays Ltd, Elcograf S.p.A.

A CIP catalogue record for this book is available from the British Library

ISBN: 978-0-241-25036-5

After the capture of Saguntum Hannibal had retired to winter quarters in New Carthage. News was brought him of the various activities in Rome and Carthage and of the decisions which had been made, so when he learned that he was himself the cause of the coming war as well as the commander-in-chief of the Carthaginian armies, he determined to act swiftly. As soon as he had completed the division and sale of the remainder of the captured material, he summoned a meeting of his Spanish troops, and addressed them as follows: 'My friends, no doubt you see as well as I do that, with all the Spanish peoples subject to our influence, one of two courses is open to us: either we must stop fighting and disband our armies, or pursue our conquests elsewhere. By doing the latter, and by seeking plunder and renown from the conquest of other countries, the Spanish peoples will reap the harvest not only of peace but of victory. Since, therefore, we are soon to fight a campaign in distant parts and nobody knows when you may see your homes and loved ones again, I have decided to grant leave of absence to any man who wishes to visit his family. Your orders are to return to duty at the beginning of spring, in order that, with God's help, we may begin a war which will fill your pockets with gold and carry your fame to the world's end.'

Most of the men were already feeling the separation from their families and looking forward sadly to a longer separation to come; so the unexpected offer of leave was very welcome. The whole winter was a time of inactivity between two periods of hard service, one completed, the other still to be faced, and the respite gave the troops fresh strength, both physical and moral, to endure again all that might be required of them. At the beginning of spring they reassembled according to orders.

After reviewing his auxiliary troops Hannibal went to Gades to pay his vows to the Tyrian Hercules in the temple there, and swore to express further obligations to that god, should his affairs prosper. His next concern was the twofold task of perfecting his offensive and defensive measures. To obviate the danger of a Roman invasion of Africa by way of Sicily while he was marching for Italy through Spain and the Gallic provinces, he took the precaution of stationing a powerful force in the island. As this necessitated reinforcements, he asked for a fresh contingent of African troops, mostly light-armed spearmen, intending to employ African troops in Spain and Spanish troops in Africa in the belief that service by each in a foreign country would provide a sort of mutual guarantee of good behaviour. He sent 13,850 targeteers to Africa together with 870 slingers from the Balearic Islands and 1,200 cavalrymen of various nationality, some to serve in different parts of Africa, some to garrison Carthage; at the same time he dispatched officers to raise troops from the states dependent upon him, with orders that 4,000 picked men should be moved to Carthage to strengthen the garrison there and also to act as hostages.

Spain moreover was not to be neglected, especially in view of the recent Roman attempt to seduce the leading men of the various Spanish peoples from their allegiance, and the defence of the country was put into the capable hands of his brother Hasdrubal. The troops under his command were mainly African: 11,850 African foot, 300 Ligurians, and 500 from the Balearics. To these were added 450 Libyphoenician horse – men of mixed blood, half Punic half African – about 1,800 Numidians and Moors from the Atlantic coast, and a small force of 200 horse from the Ilergetes in Spain. Finally, there were twenty-one elephants, to make the land-forces complete. Furthermore, as it seemed likely that the Romans might attempt to repeat their former successes by sea, Hasdrubal was given for coastal defence a fleet of fifty quinquiremes, two quadriremes, and five triremes, though of these only thirty-two quinquiremes and five triremes were actually fitted out and manned.

From Gades Hannibal returned to the army's quarters in New Carthage, and then proceeded by way of Etovissa to the river Ebro and the coast. Here, the story goes, he had a dream: a young man of godlike aspect told him he had been sent by God to guide him to Italy, and bade him follow, and in all places keep his eyes fixed upon him. Conquering his fear, he followed the divine guide, looking neither to right nor left, nor behind, until overcome by a natural human curiosity and eager to know what it was he had been forbidden to see behind him, he was unable to control his eyes any longer. He looked round, and saw a monstrous snake, gliding; and in its path trees and bushes were tumbling in dreadful ruin, while a storm-cloud loomed up behind with the crash of thunder. He asked in his dream what that fearful commotion might be and what was the meaning of the sign, and a voice said in answer that it signified the laying waste of Italy, and that he must go forward without further questioning and allow what needs must be to remain in darkness.

Encouraged by his dream he proceeded to cross the Ebro, dividing his forces into three detachments. A party had already been sent ahead to Gaul with instructions to reconnoitre the Alpine passes and to endeavour to obtain by bribes the favour of the Gallic chieftains whose territories lay along the route the army would probably follow. The force with which he crossed the river amounted to 90,000 foot and 12,000 horse. The next objectives were the Ilergetes, Bargusii, Ausetani, and the district of Lacetania on the foothills of the Pyrenees; this whole coastal area Hannibal put in charge of Hanno, to keep control of the passes between the provinces of Spain and Gaul, assigning him a force of 10,000 infantry for the purpose. The march through the passes of the Pyrenees then began.

By this time Hannibal's foreign troops had become fairly sure of his ultimate objective – the invasion of Italy; and as a result the contingent from the Carpetani, 3,000 strong, refused to proceed, in alarm, supposedly, less at the actual prospect of the fighting than of the length of the march and the well-nigh impossible passage of the Alps. To recall the deserters or to detain them by force might have adversely affected the morale of his other foreign troops, wild and undisciplined as they were, so Hannibal dismissed over 7,000 of his men whom he knew to be resentful at the prospect of the campaign ahead of them, and pretended that the deserters had also been dismissed for the same reason. Then, to prevent the undermining of discipline by idleness and delay, he proceeded forthwith to cross the Pyrenees with the rest of his troops and encamped near the town of Iliberis.

The Gauls were aware that Italy was Hannibal's objective; nevertheless the news of the subjection of the Spanish peoples beyond the Pyrenees and the occupation of their country by a powerful force so alarmed them that, in fear of being themselves reduced to slavery, a number of their tribes flew to arms and concentrated at the town of Ruscino. Hannibal, to whom the only danger in this situation seemed to be a possible delay, sent a delegation to the Gallic chieftains with instructions to tell them that he desired a conference, for which purpose either he would advance to Ruscino, or they, if they preferred, could approach Iliberis, to facilitate a meeting. He would be glad to receive them in his own camp, or – alternatively – was equally willing to come to them without hesitation, as he had entered Gaul not as an enemy but as a friend and had no intention, unless they compelled him, of drawing the sword before he was in Italy. The message was duly delivered; the Gallic chieftains promptly moved with their men to Iliberis and were easily persuaded to meet Hannibal, whereupon the presents they received soon induced them to let the Carthaginian army move on past Ruscino and through their territory without molestation.

Meanwhile, before any news had reached Rome subsequent to the report of the envoys from Massilia that Hannibal had crossed the Ebro, the Boii incited their neighbours the Insubrian Gauls to join them in revolt – almost as if Hannibal were already over the Alps. The reason for their defection was not so much their long-standing hostility to Rome as resentment at the recent planting on Gallic soil of the two settlements of Placentia and Cremona, near the river Po. Hurriedly mobilizing their forces they invaded that district and caused so much alarm and confusion that not only the rural population but even the three Roman officials who were superintending the assignment of land in the new settlement fled to Mutina, lest the walls of Placentia should prove an insufficient protection. The three officials were probably Gaius Lutatius, Gaius Servilius, and Titus Annius, though some annals have Quintus Acilius and Gaius Herennius in place of the two last, and others Publius Cornelius Asina and Gaius Papirius Maso. About Lutatius there is no discrepancy in the records. There is also some doubt about whether the envoys sent to demand reparations from the Boii were subjected to violence, or whether it was the three officials engaged upon the partition of agricultural land who were assaulted.

The Gauls were no great hands at military tactics and without any experience in siege warfare; against those shut up in Mutina they did nothing and no attempt was made to storm the defences. In these circumstances negotiations for a truce were opened – or so it was pretended. The Roman envoys, invited by the Gallic chiefs to a conference, were seized – an action which violated not only the accepted conventions of international procedure but also the specific guarantees given on the occasion – and the Gauls refused to release them unless their hostages were restored.

At the news of the envoys' plight and of the danger to Mutina and its garrison, the praetor Lucius Manlius started for the town with a relief-party. Indignation prevented proper precautions being taken. Most of the neighbourhood was uncultivated, and his road lay through woods. He had no scouts out, and the result was that he fell into a trap and suffered severe losses before he managed to struggle clear into open country. There he halted, and properly fortified his position; and his men, in spite of their losses – probably some 500 killed – recovered their morale when they found that the enemy seemed to have no heart for a concerted attack. They proceeded on their way, and so long as their route led through open country, there was no further sign of the enemy; once again, however, the moment they got into woodland, the rear of the column was attacked. Discipline went to pieces, and panic spread; six standards were lost and 700 men killed. It was not till the force emerged from the trackless and difficult wooded country that the Gauls stopped their alarming tactics and the Roman column could breathe freely. Thereafter, marching through open country, they had no difficulty in protecting themselves, and proceeded to Tannetum, a village near the Po, where they temporarily fortified a position. This, together with such provisions as could be brought down the river and the assistance of the Brixian Gauls, kept them in comparative safety against the daily increasing numbers of the enemy.

In Rome the report of this unexpected trouble, and the knowledge that the Roman government now had a war with Gaul as well as with Carthage on its hands, called for prompt action. The Senate ordered fresh troops to be raised, and instructed the praetor Gaius Atilius to march to Manlius's relief with one Roman legion and 5,000 allied troops. The enemy having dispersed in alarm, the force reached Tannetum unmolested.

At the same time Cornelius Scipio, having raised a fresh legion in place of the one which had been ordered out with the praetor, sailed from Rome with sixty warships. Coasting Etruria and Liguria, he went on past the mountains of the Salyes until he reached Massilia, where he established himself on the easternmost of the several mouths of the Rhône. He was not yet by any means sure that Hannibal had crossed the Pyrenees, though he was soon to learn that he was already preparing to cross the Rhône. As he did not know where he was likely to make contact with him, and his men had not yet recovered from the effects of their rough voyage, he took the precaution of sending out a reconnoitring party of 300 mounted troops, with local guides and supported by a Gallic contingent, to find out all they could and to watch the enemy's movements without risking an encounter. Hannibal had by now reached the territory of the Volcae, having either scared or bribed the other tribes into submission. The Volcae were a powerful people with settlements on both banks of the Rhône, but as they distrusted their ability to keep the Carthaginians from reaching the river they had decided to make use of it as a barrier to their further advance. With this in view nearly all of them had crossed over and were now holding the farther, or eastern, bank. The other tribes in the neighbourhood of the river, and even such men of the Volcae who had not abandoned their homes, Hannibal induced by the offer of presents to construct boats and rafts and to collect others from wherever they could find them. The natives themselves were only too eager to see Hannibal safely across and to have their own territory relieved as quickly as possible from the burden of his numerous army; so it was not long before an immense number of craft was assembled, big and small – the latter roughly-built boats for local use, while at the same time the Gauls set about constructing canoes hollowed from a single tree-trunk. The Carthaginian soldiers soon followed suit. The work was easy and timber abundant, and, as the only requirement was something that would float and carry a load, the result was the rapid construction of a number of rough and more or less shapeless hulls, which would at least take them and their gear across the river.

As soon as preparations were complete, they were deterred from proceeding by an assembly in force of the enemy, both horse and foot, who were thronging the farther bank of the river. To circumvent this menace, Hannibal sent Hanno, the son of Bomilcar, with a party of men, mostly Spanish, a day's journey up the river; his instructions were to start soon after dark and, on the first opportunity, to cross over, attracting as little attention as possible, and then, by an outflanking movement, to attack the enemy in the rear when occasion offered. Information was given by the Gallic guides that some twenty-five miles upstream there was a convenient place for crossing, where the river was broader and shallower as it was split into two channels by a small island. Timber was quickly cut and rafts constructed to carry the men over, together with their horses and gear, the Spanish troops making no bones about swimming across with their shields beneath them and their clothes stowed in leather bags. The rest of the force crossed on the rafts, lashed together to form a bridge. Camp was then pitched near the river bank, and the men were given a day's rest to recover from their night march and subsequent labours, their commanding officer being anxious to avoid any sort of miscarriage in the operation. Next day they got on the move again, and raised a smoke signal to indicate that they were across the river and not far away. Hannibal saw the signal, and gave immediate orders for his own men to begin their passage of the river. For the infantrymen the boats were already prepared; most of the cavalry was got across with the men swimming by the side of their horses, a line of larger craft being stationed just above them to break the force of the current, and to make easier going for the rafts and boats farther downstream. Many of the horses were attached by lines to boats' sterns, while the rest were ferried across ready saddled and bridled, for instant use by their riders on the farther side.

The Gallic warriors came surging to the river bank, howling and singing as their custom was, shaking their shields above their heads and brandishing their spears, in spite of the menace which confronted them of those innumerable hostile craft, rendered yet more alarming by the roar of the stream and the cries of the soldiers and sailors struggling to overcome the fierce current and the shouts of encouragement from their comrades awaiting their turn to cross. All this was bad enough; but suddenly, from behind, a more terrible sound assailed their ears – the triumphant shout of Hanno's men. Their camp had been captured, and a moment later Hanno himself was upon them: they were caught between two deadly menaces, the thousands of armed men landing on the river bank and a second army unexpectedly pressing upon their rear. After one fruitless attempt at active resistance they forced a way out of the trap as best they could and dispersed in confusion to their villages. Hannibal, now convinced that there was more smoke than fire in Gallic resistance, completed at leisure the passage of the river, and pitched camp.

Various methods were, I believe, employed to get the elephants across; at any rate there are differing accounts of how it was done. According to one account, the beasts were herded close to the bank, and a notably ferocious one was then goaded by his driver, who promptly plunged into the water; the furious animal pursued him as he swam for his life and so drew the rest of the herd after him. Despite their terror at finding themselves in deep water, they were all carried to the farther bank by the sheer force of the current. It is more generally thought that they were ferried across on rafts – surely a safer method, and also, to judge by the result, a more likely one. The method was to prepare a big float, 200 feet long and 50 feet wide, which was held in position against the current by a number of strong cables led to the bank upstream; it was then covered with soil like a bridge, to induce the elephants to walk on to it without fear, as if they were still on land. To this float a second raft, of the same width but only half the length, and suitable for towing across the river, was attached. The elephants, the females leading, were driven on to the float – supposing it to be a solid road – and then passed on to the raft, when the ropes which lightly attached it to the float were immediately cast off, and it was towed over to the farther bank by rowing-boats. When the first batch had been landed, others were fetched and brought over. None of the animals showed any alarm so long as they were on what seemed the solid bridge: panic began only when the raft was cast off and they found themselves being carried into deep water; it was then that they showed fright, those nearest the edge backing away from the water and causing much jostling and confusion amongst their companions, until their very terror, at the sight of water all around them, seemed to freeze them into stillness. A few completely lost their heads and fell into the water; their riders were flung off, but the beasts themselves, stabilized by their weight, struggled on bit by bit till they found shallow water, and so got ashore.

While this operation was in progress, Hannibal had sent a party of 500 Numidian horsemen to try to find out the location, strength, and intentions of the Roman force. The Numidians were met by the party of 300 Roman cavalrymen, who had been sent, as I have already mentioned, from the mouth of the Rhône to reconnoitre. The fight which followed was, in spite of the small numbers engaged, a surprisingly savage one; many were wounded and the losses in killed were about equal on both sides. It was only when the Romans had already had nearly enough that the Numidians broke and fled, and so gave them the victory. Roman losses, including the Gallic auxiliaries, amounted to 160; those of the Numidians to over 200. This preliminary skirmish might be taken as an omen of what was to come – portending final victory for Rome, but at the same time a victory far from bloodless and won only after a struggle of which the issue was to be long in doubt.

When the troops returned after this engagement to their respective commanders, Scipio could be sure of only one thing, namely that he must adjust his own movements to the actions and strategy of the enemy. Hannibal, for his part, was still hesitating between continuing his march straight into Italy, and offering battle to the first Roman force that chanced to lie in his way; he was, however, dissuaded from an immediate trial of strength with Scipio by the arrival of a delegation from the Boii with their chieftain Magalus, who promised to serve him as guides and to share his dangers, at the same time expressing the opinion that the invasion of Italy should be his sole objective, to be undertaken without any frittering away of his strength.

The rank and file of the Carthaginian army had a wholesome respect for Roman arms, as the former war was not yet forgotten; but they were much more alarmed by the prospect of the long march and, especially, of the passage of the Alps – about which stories were told dreadful enough to frighten anyone, particularly the inexperienced. In view of this, Hannibal, once he had made his decision to go ahead and to make straight for Italy, paraded his troops and delivered an address calculated to work upon their feelings by a judicious mixture of reproof and encouragement. 'What sudden panic is this,' he said, 'which has entered those breasts where fear has never been? Year after year you have fought with me, and won; and you never left Spain until all the lands and peoples between the two seas were subject to our power. When the Roman people demanded the surrender of the "criminal" – whoever it might have been – who laid siege to Saguntum, you were justly angry and crossed the Ebro bent upon obliterating the very name of Rome and setting the world free. Then, at least, none of you thought of the journey long, though it stretched from the setting to the rising sun; but now, when you can see that much the greater part of the distance is already behind you – when you have made your way through the wild tribes and over the passes of the Pyrenees, when you have tamed the violence of the mighty Rhône and crossed it in face of those countless Gallic warriors who would fain have stopped you; when, finally, you have the Alps in sight, and know that the other side of them is Italian soil: now, I repeat, at the very gateway of the enemy's country, you come to a halt – exhausted! What do you think the Alps *are*? Are they anything worse than high mountains? Say, if you will, that they are higher than the Pyrenees, but what of it? No part of earth reaches the sky; no height is insuperable to men. Moreover, the Alps are not desert: men live there, they till the ground; there are animals there, living creatures. If a small party can cross them, surely armies can? The envoys you see with us did not, in order to get over, soar into the air on wings. Moreover, their own forebears were immigrants – they were countryfolk from Italy, who often crossed these same mountains safely enough – hordes of them, with their women and children, whole peoples on the move. Surely, then, for an army of soldiers, with nothing to carry but their military gear, no waste should be too wild to cross, no hills too high to climb. Remember Saguntum, and those eight long months of toil and peril endured to the end. It is not Saguntum now, but Rome, the mightiest city of the world, you aim to conquer: how can you feel that anything, however hard, however dangerous, can make you hesitate? Why, even the Gauls once captured Rome – and you despair of being able even to get near it. Either confess, then, that you have less spirit and courage than a people you have again and again defeated during these latter days, or steel your hearts to march forward, to halt only on Mars' Field between the Tiber and the walls of Rome.'

Hannibal's words were not without effect. When he had ended, he gave the order for his men to rest and prepare themselves for the march.

The army moved on the following day. The route Hannibal chose was along the Rhône valley towards central Gaul. This was not the more direct route to the Alps, but Hannibal preferred it as the farther he got from the coast the less likely he was to encounter Roman resistance, and he had no wish for a trial of strength until he reached Italy. Four days later he was at the junction of the Isaras and the Rhône, both of which flow down from the Alps and embrace a stretch of country known as the Island. In this neighbourhood was the territory of the Allobroges, a people even in those days inferior to none in Gaul for power and fame. At the time of Hannibal's arrival the country was split by internal discord, two brothers disputing for the throne; the elder, Brancus, had been king, but an attempt was being made by his younger brother to depose him, with the support of the young nobles and the claim that might, in this case, was right. The two rivals seized the opportunity of Hannibal's presence to refer to him the decision of the quarrel, and he, acting as arbitrator, and supporting the views of the council and the leading men, restored the throne to Brancus. In recognition of this service he was assisted by a gift of provisions and supplies of all sorts, especially of clothing, which it was essential to lay in against the notorious cold of the high Alps.

The business of the Allobroges settled, Hannibal's objective was now the mountains themselves. Still avoiding the most direct route, he turned left to the territory of the Tricastini, proceeding thence past the borders of the Vocontii to the Tricorii and finding nothing to stop him until he reached the river Druentia. This Alpine stream is more awkward to cross than any other river in Gaul; in spite of its volume of water nothing can float on it, because, not being contained by banks, it is split up into a number of constantly changing channels, where the shallows and deep potholes, dangerous to a man on foot, shift from day to day; add the stones and gravel swept down by the rapid current, and it is clear that anyone who enters it will find a foothold by no means firm or safe. On this occasion the stream was swollen by rains, with the result that the crossing was a scene of extraordinary confusion, the rank and file adding to the very real and actual dangers by their own disorderly clamour and desperate haste to get over.

The consul Publius Cornelius had reached Hannibal's position on the Rhône three days too late. His troops were in battle order, and his intention was to engage immediately; but all he found was an empty encampment. As it became clear to him that Hannibal had too long a start to be easily overtaken, he rejoined his fleet, thinking that the better and safer course would be to confront Hannibal on his descent of the Alps into northern Italy. At the same time, as he was unwilling to leave his own province of Spain without a Roman force to protect it, he sent the greater part of his army there under the command of his brother Gnaeus Scipio, with instructions not only to support against Hasdrubal the Spanish peoples who were already friendly to Rome and to win others to her alliance, but also, if he could, to drive Hasdrubal from Spain altogether. He himself meanwhile returned with quite a small force to Genoa intending to defend Italy with the troops already stationed in the vicinity of the Po.

From the Druentia Hannibal advanced towards the Alps mainly through open country, and reached the foothills without encountering any opposition from the local tribes. The nature of the mountains was not, of course, unknown to his men by rumour and report – and rumour commonly exaggerates the truth; yet in this case all tales were eclipsed by the reality. The dreadful vision was now before their eyes: the towering peaks, the snow-clad pinnacles soaring to the sky, the rude huts clinging to the rocks, beasts and cattle shrivelled and parched with cold, the people with their wild and ragged hair, all nature, animate and inanimate, stiff with frost: all this, and other sights the horror of which words cannot express, gave a fresh edge to their apprehension. As the column moved forward up the first slopes, there appeared, right above their heads, ensconced upon their eminences, the local tribesmen, wild men of the mountains, who, if they had chosen to lurk in clefts of the hills, might well have sprung out from ambush upon the marching column and inflicted untold losses and disaster.

Hannibal soon ordered a halt and sent his Gallic guides forward to reconnoitre. Informed that he could not get through there, he encamped in the best stretch of fairly level ground he could find, hemmed in though it was by savagely broken rocks and precipitous cliffs. Later he learned from the same guides, whose way of life and language were much like those of the local tribesmen, and who had been able, in consequence, to listen to their deliberations, that the pass was held only in the daytime, and that at nightfall the natives dispersed to their homes. In view of this information, at dawn next morning he approached the eminences where the tribesmen were on watch as if with the intention of openly trying to force a passage through the defile during the hours of daylight. During the rest of the day he concealed his actual purpose; his men fortified the position where they had originally halted, and it was not till he was sure that the tribesmen had abandoned the heights and gone off guard that his real intention became evident. Leaving the baggage in camp with all the cavalry and most of the infantry, and kindling, for a blind, more fires than the numbers actually left in camp would justify, he assembled a force of light-armed infantrymen, all men picked for their courage and determination, swiftly cleared the defile, and established himself on the heights which the tribesmen had been holding. At dawn next morning camp was broken up and the rest of the army moved forward.

The tribesmen were beginning to muster at their usual look-out station on the heights when, to their astonishment, they saw the Carthaginian assault-troops right above their heads and already in possession of it, while another army of them was passing through along the track. The two things together were such a shock to them that for the moment they were frozen into immobility; soon, however, the sight of the enemy's own difficulties restored their confidence. In the narrow pass the marching column was rapidly losing cohesion; there was great confusion and excitement amongst the men, and still more amongst the terrified horses, so the tribesmen, in the hope that any hostile action by themselves would be enough to complete their discomfiture, came swarming down the rocky and precipitous slopes, sure-footed as they were from long familiarity with their wild and trackless terrain. The Carthaginians thus found themselves facing two enemies – the hostile tribesmen and the terrible difficulty of their position in the narrow defile. It was a case of every man for himself, and in their struggles to get clear of danger they were fighting with each other rather than with the enemy. It was the horses, more than anything else, which created havoc in the column: terrified by the din, echoing and re-echoing from the hollow cliffs and woods, they were soon out of control, while those which were struck or wounded lashed out in an agony of fear, causing serious losses both of men and gear of all descriptions. In the confusion many non-combatants, and not a few soldiers, were flung over the sheer cliffs which bounded each side of the pass, and fell to their deaths thousands of feet below; but it was worst for the pack-animals – loads and all, they went tumbling over the edge almost like falling masonry.

All this was a shocking spectacle; nevertheless Hannibal, watching from above, stayed for the moment where he was and kept his assault-troops in check, lest their joining the column should only add to the confusion. But when he saw the column break up, and realized that even to get the men through safely would not help him much if all their gear were lost, he knew it was time to act. Hurrying down from his position on the heights, he scattered the hostile tribesmen with a single charge. His arrival did, indeed, increase the confusion amongst his own men, but only for a moment; for once the enemy had fled and the track was clear, order was restored, and it was not long before the whole army, unmolested and almost in silence, was brought safely through. The chief fortified village of the district, together with the neighbouring hamlets, was then captured, and the cattle and grain taken from these places proved sufficient to feed the army for three days. As the tribesmen had learned their lesson, and the going was now comparatively easy, the army during these three days made considerable progress.

Coming to the territory of another mountain tribe, a numerous one for this sort of country, Hannibal encountered no open resistance, but fell into a cunningly laid trap. In fact he nearly succumbed to the very tactics in which he himself excelled. The elders of the fortified villages presented themselves in the guise of envoys, and declared that the wholesome example of others' suffering had taught them to prefer the friendship of the Carthaginians to the risk of learning at first hand of their military might. They were willing, in consequence, to submit to Hannibal's orders, to supply him with guides and provisions, and to offer hostages as a guarantee of their good faith. Hannibal was too cautious to take what they said at its face value, but was unwilling to reject the offer out of hand, lest a refusal should drive them into open hostility; accordingly he replied in friendly terms, accepted the hostages, and made use of the supplies the natives had offered; he then followed their guides – but with proper precautions, and by no means proceeding in loose order, as he might have done in friendly territory.

At the head of the column were the cavalry and elephants; Hannibal himself, with the pick of the infantry, brought up the rear, keeping his eyes open and alert for every contingency. Before long the column found itself on a narrowing track, one side of which was overhung by a precipitous wall of rock, and it was suddenly attacked. The natives, springing from their places of concealment, fiercely assaulted front and rear, leaping into the fray, hurling missiles, rolling down rocks from the heights above. The worst pressure was on Hannibal's rear; to meet it, his infantry faced-about – and it was clear enough that, had not the rear of the column been adequately protected, the Carthaginian losses would have been appalling. Even as it was the moment was critical, and disaster only just averted; for Hannibal hesitated to send his own division into the pass – to do so would have deprived the infantry of such support as he was himself providing for the cavalry – and his hesitation enabled the tribesmen to deliver a flank attack, cut the whole column in two, and establish themselves on the track. As a result, Hannibal, for one night, found himself cut off from his cavalry and baggage-train. Next day, however, as enemy activity weakened, a junction was effected between the two halves of the column and the defile was successfully passed, though not without losses, especially amongst the pack-animals.

Thenceforward there was no concerted opposition, the natives confining themselves to mere raids, in small parties, on front or rear, as the nature of the ground dictated, or as groups of stragglers, left behind or pressing on ahead of the column as the case might be, offered a tempting prey. The elephants proved both a blessing and a curse: for though getting them along the narrow and precipitous tracks caused serious delay, they were none the less a protection to the troops, as the natives, never having seen such creatures before, were afraid to come near them.

On the ninth day the army reached the summit. Most of the climb had been over trackless mountain-sides; frequently a wrong route was taken – sometimes through the deliberate deception of the guides, or, again, when some likely-looking valley would be entered by guess-work, without knowledge of whither it led. There was a two days' halt on the summit, to rest the men after the exhausting climb and the fighting. Some of the pack-animals which had fallen amongst the rocks managed, by following the army's tracks, to find their way into camp. The troops had indeed endured hardships enough; but there was worse to come. It was the season of the setting of the Pleiades: winter was near – and it began to snow. Getting on the move at dawn, the army struggled slowly forward over snow-covered ground, the hopelessness of utter exhaustion in every face. Seeing their despair, Hannibal rode ahead and at a point of vantage which afforded a prospect of a vast extent of country, he gave the order to halt, pointing to Italy far below, and the Po Valley beyond the foothills of the Alps. 'My men,' he said, 'you are at this moment passing the protective barrier of Italy – nay more, you are walking over the very walls of Rome. Henceforward all will be easy going – no more hills to climb. After a fight or two you will have the capital of Italy, the citadel of Rome, in the hollow of your hands.'

The march continued, more or less without molestation from the natives, who confined themselves to petty raids when they saw a chance of stealing something. Unfortunately, however, as in most parts of the Alps the descent on the Italian side, being shorter, is correspondingly steeper, the going was much more difficult than it had been during the ascent. The track was almost everywhere precipitous, narrow, and slippery; it was impossible for a man to keep his feet; the least stumble meant a fall, and a fall a slide, so that there was indescribable confusion, men and beasts stumbling and slipping on top of each other.

Soon they found themselves on the edge of a precipice – a narrow cliff falling away so sheer that even a lightly-armed soldier could hardly have got down it by feeling his way and clinging to such bushes and stumps as presented themselves. It must always have been a most awkward spot, but a recent landslide had converted it on this occasion to a perpendicular drop of nearly a thousand feet. On the brink the cavalry drew rein – their journey seemed to be over. Hannibal, in the rear, did not yet know what had brought the column to a halt; but when the message was passed to him that there was no possibility of proceeding, he went in person to reconnoitre. It was clear to him that a detour would have to be made, however long it might prove to be, over the trackless and untrodden slopes in the vicinity. But even so he was no luckier; progress was impossible, for though there was good foothold in the quite shallow layer of soft fresh snow which had covered the old snow underneath, nevertheless as soon as it had been trampled and dispersed by the feet of all those men and animals, there was left to tread upon only the bare ice and liquid slush of melting snow underneath. The result was a horrible struggle, the ice affording no foothold in any case, and least of all on a steep slope; when a man tried by hands or knees to get on his feet again, even those useless supports slipped from under him and let him down; there were no stumps or roots anywhere to afford a purchase to either foot or hand; in short, there was nothing for it but to roll and slither on the smooth ice and melting snow. Sometimes the mules' weight would drive their hoofs through into the lower layer of old snow; they would fall and, once down, lashing savagely out in their struggles to rise, they would break right through it, so that as often as not they were held as in a vice by a thick layer of hard ice.

When it became apparent that both men and beasts were wearing themselves out to no purpose, a space was cleared – with the greatest labour because of the amount of snow to be dug and carted away – and camp was pitched, high up on the ridge. The next task was to construct some sort of passable track down the precipice, for by no other route could the army proceed. It was necessary to cut through rock, a problem they solved by the ingenious application of heat and moisture; large trees were felled and lopped, and a huge pile of timber erected; this, with the opportune help of a strong wind, was set on fire, and when the rock was sufficiently heated the men's rations of sour wine were flung upon it, to render it friable. They then got to work with picks on the heated rock, and opened a sort of zigzag track, to minimize the steepness of the descent, and were able, in consequence, to get the pack-animals, and even the elephants, down it.

Four days were spent in the neighbourhood of this precipice; the animals came near to dying of starvation, for on most of the peaks nothing grows, or, if there is any pasture, the snow covers it. Lower down there are sunny hills and valleys and woods with streams flowing by: country, in fact, more worthy for men to dwell in. There the beasts were put out to pasture, and the troops given three days' rest to recover from the fatigue of their road-building. Thence the descent was continued to the plains – a kindlier region, with kindlier inhabitants.

The march to Italy was much as I have described it. The army reached the frontier in the fifth month, as some records have it, after leaving New Carthage. The crossing of the Alps took fifteen days. There is great difference of opinion about the size of Hannibal's army on his arrival in Italy; the highest recorded estimate puts it at 100,000 infantry and 20,000 cavalry; the lowest at 20,000 infantry and 6,000 cavalry. I should myself be most inclined to accept the statement of Lucius Cincius Alimentus (who mentions in his account that he was taken prisoner by Hannibal), if only he did not confuse the issue by the addition of Gallic and Ligurian troops. These included, he puts the total numbers of the army led into Italy at 80,000 infantry and 10,000 cavalry; but I think it more likely – and some writers support my view – that the Gauls and Ligurians joined voluntarily later.

Alimentus further states that he learned from Hannibal himself that, after crossing the Rhône, he lost 36,000 men and an enormous number of horses and pack-animals, having descended into Italy by way of the Ligurian Taurini, on the borders of Gallic territory. As this latter fact is generally accepted, I cannot understand why there should be any doubt about the route he followed over the Alps, or why it is often supposed that he crossed by the Pennine Alps (which got their name by the fact of his crossing) farther north. The historian Coelius Antipater says that he crossed by Mt Cremo, but neither of these routes would have brought him to the Taurini – they would have led through the territory of the hill-dwelling Salassi to the Libuan Gauls. Nor is it likely that those more northern passes into Gaul were then open; the route, especially, which leads to the Pennine Alps would have been blocked by half-German tribes, and there is another thing which anyone inclined to believe in the Pennine route might do well to consider: the fact, namely, that the Veragri, who live thereabouts, know nothing of the derivation of the name 'Pennine' from the circumstance of the 'Punic' crossing. On the contrary, they derive the name from Penninus, the divinity to whom they have consecrated a shrine on the mountain top.

Conveniently for the start of Hannibal's operations, war had broken out between the Taurini and the Insubrian Gauls. Hannibal was not, however, in a position to use his troops in armed support of either party, as they were not yet fully recovered from their tribulations – and the early stages of convalescence are often worse than the disease.

The men had become as filthy and unkempt as savages, and the sudden change from labour to leisure, from starvation to plenty, from dirt and misery to decent living had affected them in various ways. It was this that offered the consul Cornelius Scipio a chance of coming to grips with them before they were properly fit again, and for that reason, after reaching Pisae, he had hurried northward to the Po, having taken over from Manlius and Atilius a body of inexperienced troops still somewhat bewildered by their recent defeat by the Gauls. However, by the time he reached Placentia Hannibal had moved on, and had already taken by storm the chief town of the Taurini, who had refused to ally themselves with him; he might moreover have secured by intimidation the support – or even the willing support – of the Gauls in the neighbourhood of the Po, had not the consul's appearance surprised them while they were still looking round for the best moment to secede. At the same time Hannibal left the Taurini, thinking that his actual presence would induce the Gauls who had not made up their minds which side to take, to follow him.

The rival armies were now almost within sight of each other. So far neither of the commanders fully knew the quality of his antagonist, yet they confronted each other not without a certain feeling of mutual respect. The name of Hannibal had been a famous one in Rome even before the destruction of Saguntum; and Hannibal for his part could not but believe in the genius of Scipio simply because he, of all men, had been chosen to oppose him. Moreover, the feats recently performed by each increased the other's admiration – Hannibal's daring and successful passage of the Alps, Scipio's masterly speed in meeting his antagonist in Italy, after being left behind in Gaul.

Scipio was the first to cross the Po. He took up a position on the river Ticinus, and, before advancing to battle, addressed his troops in the following hortatory words.

'My men,' he said, 'there would be no call for a speech from me, if I were leading into action the army which I commanded in Gaul. The cavalrymen who so splendidly routed the enemy horse on the Rhône would need no words of exhortation; nor would those legions with whom I pursued Hannibal and wrung from him what was as good as a victory – the admission, namely, that he was running away and refusing battle. But, as things are, that army, levied for Spanish service, is doing its duty, under the command of my deputy, my brother Gnaeus, in the country where the Senate and people of Rome wished it to serve. I, for my part, have freely offered myself for service here, so that you might have a consul to lead you against Hannibal and the Carthaginians. You and I are as yet unacquainted with each other; so my words must be few.

'My men, let me tell you of the sort of warfare you must expect: it will be against an enemy you defeated in the last war both on land and at sea; an enemy from whom you have exacted tribute for twenty years; an enemy from whom you took Sicily and Sardinia as prizes of war. You, therefore, will enter upon it with the high hearts of victors, they in the despondency of beaten men. Nay more, their readiness to fight at all is due not to courage but necessity – unless you imagine that an enemy who declined combat when his army was still intact, has better hopes of success now that he has lost two thirds of his troops during the passage of the Alps. Perhaps you will answer that though they are few they are nevertheless brave and strong – that they are irresistible fighters. Nonsense! They are the ghosts and shadows of men; already half dead with hunger, cold, dirt, and neglect; all their strength has been crushed and beaten out of them by the Alpine crags. Cold has dried them up, snowstorms have frozen their sinews stiff, their hands and feet are frost-bitten, their horses lamed and enfeebled; and they have not a weapon amongst them which is not damaged or broken. What an army! Why, you will not be facing an enemy at all, but only the dregs of what once were men. My chief fear is that we shall have to admit that it was the Alps, not you, who conquered Hannibal. Ah well! perhaps it was right that the gods, without human aid, should have fought the first stages of a war with treaty-breakers like these; we who – after heaven – have suffered from their treachery have the duty only of bringing that war to its conclusion.

'I am not afraid that you will suspect me of concealing my real feelings, and of exaggerating the facts merely to encourage you. I was at liberty, had I wished, to go with my army into Spain, and I had already started thither. In Spain – my own allotted sphere of action – I should have had my brother to advise me and to share my perils; I should have had an easier campaign on my hands, with Hasdrubal instead of Hannibal as my antagonist; nevertheless, as I was sailing along the Gallic coast I had news of Hannibal, and landed; I ordered my cavalry forward, I moved up to the Rhône. The cavalry was offered a chance of action – I seized it, and won. Hannibal's infantry I could not overtake on land – like an army in flight they were going too fast; so I returned to my fleet and with all possible speed accomplished the long voyage and the long march, to meet him here at the foot of the Alps. Does it look as if, while trying to escape a fight with this terrible foe, I have now encountered him accidentally? Is it not more likely that I have deliberately planted myself in his path, and am challenging him to fight? I want to find out if during these last twenty years the earth has suddenly produced a new race of Carthaginians – or if they are still like those whom you ransomed at Eryx for eighteen denarii a head. I want to know if this man Hannibal can substantiate his claim to be the rival of Hercules – that world-traveller and mighty man of valour – or if he has just been left by his father as a tax-paying underling, or even as a slave, of the Roman people. Were he not haunted by his guilt over Saguntum, he might well reflect upon his conquered country, or at least upon his own father and family – upon the treaties signed by the hand of Hamilcar, who at the bidding of a Roman consul marched his garrison down from their fortress on Mt Eryx, and in grief and rage accepted the harsh conditions – the evacuation of Sicily and the payment of a tribute to Rome – imposed on his vanquished countrymen:

'For these reasons I expect you to fight not only with your usual valour, but with the added force of indignation and anger, as if you saw your own slaves coming suddenly in arms against you. We might, on Eryx, have starved the enemy to death – the most terrible of punishments; we might have sent our victorious fleet to Africa, and in a couple of days blotted Carthage from the map without a blow in return.

Instead, we listened to their cries for mercy, and pardoned them. We lifted the blockade, and made peace; and as if that were not enough, we gave them our protection when they were involved in the African war.

'And now, they repay our generosity by following a young commander drunk with ambition, and coming to attack our country. Would that the coming struggle were for your glory only, and not also for your lives! But you must fight not, as once, for the possession of Sicily and Sardinia, but in defence of Italy. There is no other army behind us, to stop Hannibal if we fail; there are no more Alps to give us time to mobilize fresh defences. It is here, my men, that we must make our stand, as if we were fighting before the walls of Rome. I call upon each one of you to remember that he is protecting, not his own body, but the lives of his wife and little children – and then to go beyond his personal cares in the full realization that the eyes of the Senate and people of Rome are upon us now. On our hands and hearts today will depend the future fortune of that great City and of the Roman Empire.'

Unlike Scipio, Hannibal thought that deeds would be a better encouragement to his men than words. He formed his troops into a circle, and had some prisoners, whom he had captured in the mountains, brought into the middle of it in chains. Gallic weapons were laid on the ground in front of them, and an interpreter was told to ask if any of them would be willing to fight in single combat if he were released from his chains and offered a horse, together with the weapons, as the prize of victory. Every one of them declared himself eager to fight, and when lots were cast there was not a man but hoped that the luck would come his way. When it did, the lucky one leapt exultantly upon the sword and shield, glorying in the congratulations of his comrades and dancing the wild dances of his people. During the actual combats, the feeling both amongst the prisoners themselves and the Carthaginian spectators was such that the fortune of the victors seemed hardly more worthy of praise than the brave death of the defeated.

It proved a stimulating spectacle, and when several pairs had fought the parade was dismissed. Later Hannibal called another meeting of all ranks, and addressed them (we are told) in the following words:

'My soldiers, just now, as you were watching other men's fate, you were not unmoved; only think with similar feelings of what is in store for yourselves, and victory is already in our hands. What you have seen was more than a spectacle for your entertainment: it was a sort of image, or allegory, of your own condition. It may indeed be that fate has laid upon you heavier chains and harsher necessities than upon those prisoners of ours. North and south the sea hems you in; you have not a single ship even to escape in with your lives; facing you is the Po, a greater and more turbulent river than the Rhône. Behind you is the Alpine barrier, which even in the freshness and flower of your strength you almost failed to cross. Here then, where you have first come face to face with the enemy, you must conquer or die. But have courage! Circumstances compel you to fight; but those same circumstances offer you in the event of victory nobler rewards than a man might pray for, even from the immortal gods. The prize would be great enough, were we only to recover by the strength of our hands the islands of Sicily and Sardinia which our fathers lost; but all the heaped wealth of Rome, won in her long career of conquest, will be yours; those rich possessions – yes, and the possessors too. Forward then, and win this splendid prize! and with God's blessing draw your swords! You have chased cattle long enough in the wild mountains of Lusitania and Celtiberia, with nothing to show for the long years of toil and danger; since then you have travelled far, over mountains, across rivers, through peoples in arms, and it is time that you fought a campaign with money in it and all good things, and earned a rich reward for your efforts. Here Fortune has granted you an end to your sweat and tears; and here she will pay you worthily for your long service in the field. You need not imagine that victory will be as hard to win as the fame of our antagonists might suggest. Fortune is fickle: often a despised enemy has fought to the death, and a feather in the scale has brought defeat to famous nations and their kings. Take away the blinding brilliance of the name, and in what can the Romans be compared with you? To say nothing of your twenty years of brave and successful service in the field, you have come to this place from the Pillars of Hercules, from the Atlantic Ocean and the farthest limits of the world, thrusting your victorious way through all the wild and warlike nations of Spain and Gaul; and now you will be facing an army of raw recruits, beaten this very summer to its knees and penned in by the Gauls – an army and a commander still strangers to one another. And what a commander! Am I to compare myself with him – that six months' general who abandoned his own troops – when I, born and bred on active service, in my illustrious father's tent, subdued Spain and Gaul and vanquished not only the wild Alpine tribes but – a much harder task – the Alps themselves? Show Scipio now the soldiers of Rome and of Carthage without their standards, and I would wager he couldn't tell which were his own. Now as for me, my men, there is not one of you who has not with his own eyes seen me strike a blow in battle; I have watched and witnessed your valour in the field, and your acts of courage I know by heart, with every detail of when and where they took place: and this, surely, is not a thing of small importance. I was your pupil before I was your commander; I shall advance into the line with soldiers I have a thousand times praised and rewarded; and the enemy we shall meet are raw troops with a raw general, neither knowing anything of the other.

'Wherever I look, I see high hearts and strong arms: I see my veteran infantry, my cavalry, native and Numidian, all drawn from nations of noble blood; I see my brave and loyal allies; and, lastly, you, my fellow countrymen of Carthage, whom just resentment as well as patriotism has inspired to fight. We are the aggressors, we the invaders of Italy – and for that reason shall fight with a courage and audacity corresponding to our hopes – with the well-known confidence of him who strikes the first blow. Anger, the sense of unmerited injury, will spur you on and give you added fire: remember how they demanded the surrender of my person – of me, your commander – as a criminal, and later of every man amongst you who might have fought at Saguntum. Had you been given up they would certainly have put you to death with the cruellest tortures. The Romans are a proud and merciless people; they claim to make the world their own and subject to their will. They demand the right to dictate to us who our friends should be and who our enemies. They circumscribe our liberties, barring us in behind barriers of rivers or mountains beyond which we may not pass – but they do not themselves observe the limits they have set. "Do not cross the Ebro," they say; "keep your hands off Saguntum." "But is Saguntum on the Ebro?" you say. "Then don't go anywhere – stay where you are!"

'"It is not enough," you say, "that you steal our ancient possessions Sicily and Sardinia. Must you have Spain too? If I abandon Spain, you will cross into Africa." *Will*, indeed! Why, of the two consuls elected this year they have already sent one to Africa, the other to Spain. We have nothing left in the world but what we can win with our swords. Timidity and cowardice are for men who can see safety at their backs – who can retreat without molestation along some easy road and find refuge in the familiar fields of their native land; but they are not for you: you must be brave; for you there is no middle way between victory and death – put all hope of it from you, and either conquer, or, should fortune hesitate to favour you, meet death in battle rather than in flight.

'Think on these things; carry them printed on your minds and hearts. Then – I repeat – success is already yours. God has given to man no sharper spur to victory than contempt of death.'

Such were the two orations with which the rival commanders sought to inflame the spirit of their men.

Scipio's first move was to throw a bridge over the Ticinus

and to construct a blockhouse to protect it. Hannibal, while the work was in progress, sent a squadron of Numidian cavalry, 500 strong, under Maharbal to devastate the land of the local tribesmen who were friendly to Rome, with special instructions to spare, so far as possible, Gallic property and to urge the Gallic chieftains to turn against their Roman masters. When the bridge was finished the Roman force crossed and took up a position five miles from Victumulae in the territory of the Insubres. Hannibal's army lay close by, and when he saw that a battle was imminent he hurriedly recalled Maharbal's squadron and summoned another meeting of his troops. This time, in the belief that all his previous warnings and exhortations had been insufficient if he was to get the best out of his men, he promised certain specific rewards, in order further to arouse their fighting spirit. One promise was the gift of land either in Italy, Africa, or Spain, according to choice, the land to be free of tax for the recipient and his children; secondly, he was prepared to give an equivalent in money to whoever preferred it; thirdly, members of allied nations who wished to become Carthaginian citizens would be enabled to do so; lastly, if any of them preferred to return home, he promised to do his utmost to secure their position there, so that they should not wish to see the situation of any of their countrymen exchanged for their own. He further offered their liberty to slaves who had accompanied their masters on service, promising the masters two slaves for each one thus lost. To prove the genuineness of these offers, taking a lamb in his left hand and a stone in his right, he prayed to Jupiter and the other gods that, if he broke his word, they would serve him as he was about to serve the lamb – whereupon he crushed the animal's head with the stone. The gesture succeeded: the entire army, convinced that God himself was now the guarantor of their hopes, and feeling that nothing delayed the realization of them except the fact that they were not yet fighting, as one man with one voice demanded instant action.

The Romans, for their part, were by no means so eager to engage. For one thing, they had been alarmed recently by certain ominous events: a wolf had got into the camp, mauled those he met, and escaped unhurt; and bees had swarmed on a tree which overhung the commander's tent. Proper steps were taken to avert these omens, and then Scipio moved: advancing with his cavalry and light-armed spearmen to reconnoitre the enemy's position and get what information he could at close range about the nature and strength of their forces, he unexpectedly fell in with Hannibal and his own cavalry who were out on a similar reconnaissance. At first neither force was aware of the other, and for each the first sign of an approaching enemy was the cloud of dust raised by the movement of horses and men over the dry ground. Both columns halted and prepared to engage.

Scipio posted his spearmen and Gallic cavalry in the front line, with the Roman troops and the pick of the allies in support. The native (or 'bridled') cavalry formed the centre of Hannibal's line, with the Numidian horse on the wings. Hardly had the battle-cry been raised, when Scipio's spearmen broke and ran, hoping to save themselves amongst the support-troops in the rear. For a time the respective cavalry formations maintained an equal struggle, until Scipio's squadrons found themselves seriously handicapped by the spearmen – infantry troops – who had got mixed up with them. Many fell from their horses, or dismounted to bring aid to hard-pressed comrades; to a great extent things were assuming the aspect of an infantry battle, when suddenly the Numidian horse, which had formed the enemy wings, executed a circling movement and appeared in the Roman rear. It was a severe blow to the Roman morale, and the situation was made worse by the fact that Scipio was wounded, and saved from death only by the intervention of his young son. This was the boy who was later to win the glory of bringing the war to a successful conclusion, and by his splendid victory over Hannibal and the Carthaginians to earn the title of Africanus.

The rout of the spearmen – the first object of the Numidians' attack – was pretty complete; the cavalry, on the other hand, maintained cohesion, forming a screen round the wounded consul whom they protected with their persons as well as with their swords, and bringing him into camp without any sort of confusion and in perfectly good order. Coelius Antipater gives the honour of saving Scipio's life to a Ligurian slave; I myself prefer to believe that it was his son, basing my belief on the testimony of the greater number of historians, and on popular tradition.

This was the first battle of the war, and it showed clearly that in cavalry the Carthaginians had the advantage. From that it followed that open country, like that between the Po and the Alps, was not suitable for effective Roman resistance. Accordingly next night the order was given to pack up as quietly as possible and break camp. All speed was made towards the Po, Scipio's intention being to get his men across on the floating bridge, which had not yet been broken up, without the confusion inevitably caused by enemy pursuit. The army reached Placentia before Hannibal knew it had left the Ticinus; he succeeded, however, in capturing some 600 stragglers who were still on the hither bank of the Po, engaged in breaking up the floating bridge – and taking their time over it. He could not cross by it himself, because the floats at either end had already been cast off and the whole thing was drifting downstream. Coelius Antipater tells us that Mago with the cavalry and Spanish infantry promptly swam the river, using a line of elephants to check the force of the current, while Hannibal got the rest of his troops across by means of a ford higher up. But anyone who knows the Po will find this account hard to believe: it is unlikely that mounted troops could get the better of the very strong current without losing their horses and gear, even though the Spaniards may all have swum across on bladders. Moreover, to find a ford suitable for the crossing of a heavily laden army would have meant a long trek lasting many days. I prefer to follow the authorities who state that within two days they found, not without difficulty, a place where a bridge of rafts could be constructed, and that the light-armed Spanish cavalry under Mago was sent over it in advance of the main body. Hannibal waited in the neighbourhood of the river while he received delegations from the Gauls, and crossed later with his heavier infantry, Mago, meanwhile, proceeding towards the enemy at Placentia, a day's march from the Po. A few days later Hannibal fortified a position six miles from Placentia, and the day after that deployed his force in sight of the Romans and offered battle.

During the following night there was an unpleasant incident in the Roman camp – disturbing rather than actually serious: it was the work of the Gallic auxiliaries, some 2,000 of whom with 200 of their mounted troops killed the sentries on duty at the gates and deserted to Hannibal. Hannibal gave them a friendly reception, raised their hopes of rich rewards, and sent them off to their various communities with instructions to try to turn popular feeling against Rome. Scipio was afraid that the murder of the sentries might prove to be the signal for a universal Gallic revolt, and that the whole people might catch the infection and rush to arms; so in spite of the fact that his wound was still troublesome, late the following night he quietly broke camp and proceeded towards the river Trebia where he took up a fresh position on higher ground in hilly country, less suitable for cavalry to manoeuvre in. This time he was less successful in escaping observation; Hannibal sent his Numidians after him, followed by his whole cavalry force, and would certainly have caused havoc in Scipio's rear, had not the Numidians allowed their greed for plunder to divert them into his abandoned camp. There they ransacked everything but found nothing to compensate for the delay. Valuable time had been lost, and the enemy meanwhile had slipped through their fingers. When they saw that the Romans had already crossed the Trebia and were marking out their new camp, they did succeed in killing a few stragglers who had not yet got over the river.

Scipio's wound had been made intolerably painful by the jolting it had received on the march; for this reason, added to his wish to wait for his colleague, who he now knew had been recalled from Sicily, he determined to fortify a permanent defensive position on the safest spot he could find near the river. Hannibal took up his own position close by; he was elated by the success of his cavalry, but at the same time anxious about his supplies: indeed, the problem of supplies was growing every day more acute, as he never had anything prepared in advance and was marching through enemy territory. In these circumstances he sent a demand to the little settlement of Clastidium, where the Romans had amassed a large store of grain. Hannibal was preparing to assault the place, when a good chance appeared of its being betrayed to him – as indeed it was, and for the insignificant sum of 400 gold pieces. The commander of the garrison who accepted this bribe was one Dasius, from Brundisium. Clastidium was Hannibal's granary while his troops remained on the Trebia. Wishing, at the beginning of his campaign, to gain a reputation for clemency, he used no harsh measures against the prisoners who had given themselves up with the garrison.

On the Trebia the war by land had come to a temporary halt; but meanwhile both before and after the arrival of the consul Sempronius there had been activity around Sicily and the islands off the Italian coast. Twenty quinquiremes with a thousand fighting troops had been sent from Carthage to raid the coast; nine of them made the Liparae islands, eight Vulcan Islands, while three were swept off their course into the Straits. They were seen from Messana, and Hiero,

King of Syracuse, who was awaiting the Roman consul there, dispatched twelve warships against them. The three quinquiremes offered no resistance, and were captured and brought into the harbour at Messana. It was learned from the captured crews that, in addition to the twenty ships of their own fleet, another squadron, of thirty-five quinquiremes, was on its way to Sicily, to raise trouble there amongst the former friends of Carthage. The primary objective of this second fleet was Lilybaeum, and, presumably, it had been wrecked on the Aegates during the same spell of bad weather which had scattered the first fleet. Hiero sent a written report of this information to the praetor Marcus Aemilius, who was in charge of affairs in Sicily, and urged him to hold Lilybaeum with a strong garrison. At the same time military officers were sent to the various neighbouring communities with orders to keep careful watch; above all, Lilybaeum was to be held, and in addition to these preparations a general order was issued to the effect that the naval allies should stock their vessels with ten days' cooked food, and, at the given signal, instantly embark. Further, watch was to be kept from look-outs all along the coast for the approach of the enemy fleet. The Carthaginians intended to reach Lilybaeum just before dawn, and for that reason had deliberately lingered on the way; but since they were approaching under sail and the moon was still up they were spotted some way off-shore, and the signal was immediately given from the look-outs. At the same time there was a call to arms in the town, and the ships were manned. Some of the troops were stationed on the walls and at the gates, some ordered to serve with the fleet. The Carthaginians soon saw that they had lost the advantage of surprise, so until day-break they lay off the harbour and employed the interval in stowing their sails and preparing their ships for battle. Then, as soon as it was light, they withdrew farther off-shore, to have open water to fight in and to enable the enemy fleet to get out of the harbour without obstruction. The Romans, for their part, were no less eager to engage, as the number and quality of their men gave them as much confidence as the memory of past actions in those same waters. Once they were in the open sea, the object of the Romans was to fight it out at close quarters as soon as might be; but not so their antagonists, who employed elusive tactics, relying on sea-manship rather than brute force and preferring to pit ship against ship instead of man against man. For the Carthagin-ian fleet, though well manned, carried few soldiers, with the result that when one of their vessels was grappled by an enemy, she was at a serious disadvantage in mere fighting strength. Once this became apparent, the disparity in the numbers of the fighting personnel was as great a tonic to the Romans as it was a discouragement to their adversaries. Seven Carthaginian ships were quickly surrounded; the rest made off. 1,700 soldiers and sailors were taken prisoner, amongst them three Carthaginians of noble rank. The Roman fleet suffered no damage, except for one ship which was holed, but managed to get back into harbour.

Before the news of this battle was known in Messana, the consul Sempronius arrived in the town. At the entrance to the straits Hiero met him with a fleet in battle order, went aboard his ship, and congratulated him on his safe arrival with his army and fleet, adding his good wishes for a successful expedition into Sicily. He then gave him a full account of the conditions there and of the Carthaginian designs, and promised the people of Rome assistance as loyal as he had rendered them when he was a young man during the first Punic War. He offered to supply the consul's legionaries and the naval allies with provisions and clothing free of charge, adding that Lilybaeum and the maritime communities were in great danger, and that to some of them a change would be not unwelcome. In view of this Sempronius determined to sail to Lilybaeum without a moment's delay. Hiero and his fleet accompanied him, and on the way thither news was brought them of the battle at Lilybaeum and the defeat and capture of the enemy ships.

Arrived at the town, Sempronius dismissed Hiero and the royal fleet, left the praetor to guard the Sicilian coast, and sailed for Malta, which was in Carthaginian hands. Hamilcar, the son of Gisgo, commander of the island's garrison, surrendered with nearly 2,000 men, and the island and town passed into Roman control. A few days later Sempronius returned to Lilybaeum, where his prisoners of war, together with those taken by the praetor, with the exception of the noblemen amongst them, were sold at public auction.

Enough now seemed to have been done to secure the eastern parts of Sicily, so Sempronius crossed to the Vulcan Islands where a Carthaginian squadron was said to be stationed. No enemy was, however, found there, for the squadron had already sailed for Italy and was, at that moment, threatening the town of Vibo after heavy and destructive raids on its territory. News of these raids was brought to Sempronius on his way back to Sicily, and at the same time he received letters from the Senate reporting Hannibal's descent into Italy and instructing him to proceed at the first possible moment to the assistance of Scipio.

Sempronius now had a good deal on his hands, and had to act promptly. His army he sent by sea to Ariminum on the Adriatic; to his second-in-command Pomponius he assigned twenty-five warships for the defence of Vibo and the Italian coast, and manned a fleet of fifty ships for the praetor Aemilius. Then, having settled affairs in Sicily, he sailed with ten ships along the Italian coast to Ariminum, whence he proceeded with his army and joined Scipio on the Trebia.

The whole military strength of Rome, and both consuls, were now facing Hannibal. It was therefore clear that unless that strength proved adequate, there was no hope of saving the Roman dominion. None the less, counsels were divided: one consul influenced, no doubt, by his wound and by his ill success in the cavalry engagement, urged caution and delay; the other, feeling, as he did, fresh and ready for anything, demanded instant action. The Gallic tribes between the Trebia and the Po were, in the present circumstances, sitting on the fence: a struggle being imminent between two mighty nations, they were unwilling to declare their allegiance outright, and looked for the favour of the winning side. The Romans accepted readily enough this attitude, provided no actually hostile move was made, but Hannibal, on the contrary, violently resented it, urging that it was the Gauls themselves who had invited him into Italy to liberate them. His indignation against them, combined with the need to get provisions for his men, induced him to send out a force of 2,000 infantry and 1,000 cavalry, mostly Numidians with an admixture of Gauls, to raid the whole district as far as the Po. The Gauls, unable to resist, were driven by this act of aggression to make up their minds; accordingly they at once turned their sympathies towards the party they hoped would defend them, sent a delegation to Roman headquarters and begged aid for their unfortunate country which was suffering only for its inhabitants' excessive loyalty to Rome. Scipio, however, found the request untimely, and disliked the matter of it; he had no reason to trust the Gauls, remembering, as he did, their many acts of treachery, in particular, not to mention others which time might have obliterated, the recent perfidy of the Boii. Sempronius, on the other hand, expressed the opinion that to offer assistance to the first who asked for it would prove the strongest possible bond for keeping the Gallic tribes loyal to Rome. Then, while his colleague was still hesitating, he dispatched his own cavalry, supported by about a thousand infantry spearmen, with orders to protect Gallic territory on the other side of the Trebia. This force surprised Hannibal's raiders while they were scattered about over the countryside and mostly quite unfit for action as they were loaded with plunder and in no sort of order. They were thrown into complete confusion, many were killed and the remnants driven in flight right up to the outposts of the Carthaginian camp. From the camp the enemy came pouring out in force, and Sempronius's men were compelled to retire, until with the arrival of reinforcements they were able to renew the offensive. After that there was a ding-dong struggle, the Romans now advancing, now giving ground. It ended with the honours more or less even, though report favoured, on the whole, a Roman victory.

To Sempronius, however, there was no doubt about the matter at all. He was beside himself with delight. He had won a famous victory – and with his cavalry, the very arm in which Scipio had suffered defeat. He was convinced that the morale of the troops was now fully restored; that there was not a man apart from his colleague who wished to delay a general engagement. As for Scipio, it was his mind that was sick rather than his body – the mere memory of his wound made him shrink from the thought of blood and battle. But because one man was sick, was that a reason for the rest to behave like dotards? No, no: further procrastination and shilly-shallying were out of the question. Were they waiting for a third consul and yet another army? The enemy camp was on Italian soil – almost within sight of Rome; the enemy objective was not the recovery of Sicily and Sardinia, nor of Spain north of the Ebro – it was the expulsion of the Romans from the land where they had been born and bred. 'Can you not hear,' he cried, 'the groans of our fathers who were wont to fight around the walls of Carthage, at the sight of their sons cowering here, in Italy, behind their defences, though two consuls and two consular armies are in the field? What would those brave men feel at the thought of all the country between the Alps and the Apennines being controlled by Hannibal?'

So Sempronius went on, urging his point of view by the sick-bed of his colleague and passionately haranguing the officers at headquarters as if addressing the troops. An additional reason for his urgency was, no doubt, the approach of the consular elections; for he had no desire that the fighting should be put off until new consuls were in control, and he himself, while his colleague lay sick, should lose the chance of gaining the glory. Scipio continued to protest, but to no purpose; the order was given to prepare for action without delay.

Hannibal was well aware of what the proper Roman strategy ought to have been, and he had hardly dared to hope that the consuls would make any rash or ill-considered move. Now, however, that facts had confirmed the report that one of them was a proud and passionate man, rendered even more so by his recent success against the raiders, he was convinced that luck was with him and that a battle was imminent. He took every possible measure to ensure that he should not lose his chance; now was the moment, while the Roman troops were still raw, and the better of their two commanders was still incapacitated by his wound. The Gauls moreover were still full of fight, and he knew that thousands of them would lose their enthusiasm for his cause in proportion as they were drawn further and further from their homes. For these and similar reasons he both expected that a fight was coming, and was determined, should the Romans hold back, to provoke one; accordingly, when his Gallic spies (it was safer to use Gauls in this capacity, as they were serving in both camps) reported that the Romans were ready for action, he began to look around for a suitable place to set a trap.

Between the armies was the stream, running between high banks and edged for some distance by a dense growth of marsh plants, together with the brambles and scrub which usually cover waste ground. Hannibal rode round on his horse minutely examining the terrain, and when he found a place which afforded adequate concealment for cavalry, he summoned his brother Mago. 'This,' he said, 'is the spot you must occupy. Choose a hundred men from the infantry, and a hundred from the cavalry, and bring them to me early tonight. Meanwhile the troops may rest.' The staff meeting was then dismissed, and soon Mago reported with the men he had picked. 'I can see,' said Hannibal, 'that you have brought me some tough fellows; but as you will all need quantity as well as quality, I want each of you to select nine others like yourselves from the cavalry squadrons and infantry companies. Mago will show you where to set your trap. The enemy, you will find, has no eye for this sort of stratagem.'

Mago's thousand horse and thousand foot were in this way sent off, and Hannibal issued orders to the Numidian cavalry to cross the Trebia at dawn, advance to the enemy position, and lure him to engage by an attack with missiles on his guard-posts; then, once the fight was on, they were to give ground gradually and so draw him to cross the river. The orders to the commanders of other units, infantry and cavalry, were to see that all their men had a good meal, after which they were to arm, saddle their horses, and await the signal.

Sempronius was thirsting for action: to meet the Numidians' raid on his guard-posts he at once led out his whole cavalry force – the arm in which he felt the greatest confidence; these were followed first by 6,000 infantry and finally by the entire army, and stationed in the spot previously determined upon.

There, between Alps and Apennines, it was a snowy winter's day, and the cold was increased by the proximity of rivers and marsh; men and horses had left the shelter of camp without a moment's warning – they had eaten nothing, taken no sort of precautions against the cold. There was not a spark of warmth in their bodies; and the nearer they approached the chilling breath of the water, the more bitterly cold it became. But worse was to come, for when in pursuit of the Numidians they actually entered the river – it had rained in the night and the water was up to their breasts – the cold so numbed them that after struggling across they could hardly hold their weapons. In fact, they were exhausted and, as the day wore on, hunger was added to fatigue.

Meanwhile Hannibal's troops were warming themselves by great fires in front of their tents. Rations of oil had been distributed for the men to rub themselves with, to keep them supple; they had all breakfasted at leisure; so that when word came that the Romans were across the river, it was a fresh and eager army that ran to its stations in the line.

In the van of his force Hannibal posted the Baliares and the light-armed foot, about 8,000 strong; supporting them were the heavier infantry – the flower of his troops. On the wings were 10,000 mounted troops, with the elephants beyond them – half on the right, half on the left. Sempronius posted his cavalry on the flanks of his infantry – having recalled them for the purpose; for in their disorderly chase after the Numidian raiding-party they had received an unexpected check from a sudden rally of the enemy. The total

Roman strength at the beginning of this battle was 18,000 legionaries, 20,000 allied troops of the Latin name, and certain contingents provided by the Cenomani, the only Gallic nation to remain loyal.

The action was opened by Hannibal's Baliares. They were met by the superior weight of the Roman legionaries and quickly withdrawn to the wings, where they greatly increased the pressure on the Roman cavalry, which was already fighting against odds – for they were tired men, while their antagonists were fresh, and more than double their number. Now, however, on top of that, the Baliares almost overwhelmed them with a cloud of javelins. The elephants, too, on the extreme wings caused widespread confusion, as the horses were terrified by the sight and smell of these strange beasts they had never seen before. As for the infantry, the Roman foot showed no lack of spirit, but they were physically weak compared with the enemy, who had entered the fight refreshed with food and rest, unlike themselves, half frozen as they were, and faint with hunger. None the less sheer courage might have carried them through if they had had only the Carthaginian infantry to contend with; but as it was, the Baliares, after the repulse of the Roman mounted troops, were attacking them on the flanks with missiles, and the elephants had by now forced a way right into their line. Finally, Mago and his Numidians, once the line had – all unaware – moved forward beyond their place of concealment, appeared suddenly in their rear with almost shattering effect. Yet even in this terrible situation the Roman line for some time held firm – even, what was least of all to be expected, against the elephants.

The light-armed foot, specially brought in to deal with them, drove them off with their javelins, followed up, and pierced them again in the soft skin under their tails. Under this treatment the brutes were getting out of hand and looked like turning in panic against their own masters, so Hannibal had them removed from the centre and transferred to the left wing, against the Gallic auxiliaries. The auxiliaries promptly broke and fled, thus adding a fresh cause of alarm for the hard-pressed Romans.

In these circumstances a body of some 10,000 Romans – who were now completely encircled – took the only way of escape they could find and hacked a passage with the edge of the sword right through the African centre, supported, as it was, by its allied Gallic contingents. The river barred the way back to camp, and it was raining so hard that they could not see at what point in the mêlée they could best help their friends, so they took the shortest route to Placentia. Subsequently a number of other groups, at various points, succeeded in breaking out; those who made for the river were either drowned or cut down as they hesitated on the brink; others, scattered in flight over the countryside, made for Placentia on the tracks of the retreating column. A few, emboldened by sheer terror of death by the sword to plunge into the water, got across and reached the camp.

Rain, sleet, and intolerable cold carried off many of the pack-animals and nearly all the elephants. At the river bank the Carthaginians ceased their pursuit, and on their return to camp the men were so benumbed with cold that they could hardly feel pleasure in their victory. Accordingly the following night they allowed the garrison in Scipio's camp and most of the remaining troops to cross the Trebia on rafts unmolested: either they were unaware of the movement because of the noise of the torrential rain, or else too exhausted for further effort, and suffering from wounds, as many were, they pretended to have noticed nothing. Scipio led his force quietly to Placentia. There was no opposition. From Placentia he crossed the Po and proceeded to Cremona, to spare one town the heavy burden of two armies wintering in it.

In Rome the news of this disastrous defeat caused such panic that people fancied that at any moment Hannibal would be at the city gates. There was no hope, it seemed, nothing to help them defend the gates and walls from assault. One consul had been beaten at the Ticinus, the other recalled from Sicily, and now the two together, with the combined force of both consular armies, had been defeated too. What other commanders, what other troops could be summoned to their defence? Such was the state of feeling when Sempronius himself arrived in Rome. His journey had been hazardous in the extreme: raiding parties of the Carthaginian horse were all over the countryside, and he had managed to come through by sheer audacity, without any fixed plan or hope of resisting if he were recognized. Once in Rome, he presided at the consular elections – the one essential thing in the present circumstances still to be done – and returned to Placentia. The new consuls were Gnaeus Servilius and Gaius Flaminius.

Even in their winter quarters the Romans were not unmolested. Numidian raiders were constantly on the warpath, and – in the wilder and rougher regions – Celtiberian and

Lusitanian as well. All supply-routes were consequently closed, except for what could be brought by boat up the Po.

Near Placentia there was an important trading-post, well fortified and strongly guarded, which Hannibal planned to surprise. He knew that his best chance of success lay in concealing his design, so with a force of mounted and light-armed troops he approached the place under cover of darkness. But the sentries on guard saw him, and such a din immediately arose from inside the fortress that it could be heard even in Placentia. Just before dawn the consul arrived on the scene with a squadron of horse, in advance of the legionaries who had orders to follow in battle array. Meanwhile the mounted troops of either side engaged each other, and in the course of the skirmish Hannibal was wounded and had to leave the field. This was a severe blow to the enemy morale and contributed, no doubt, to the successful defence of the fortress. After a few days' rest, and before his wound was properly healed, Hannibal proceeded to attack Victumulae, another trading-post which the Romans had fortified during the war with the Gauls. The place had subsequently become populous, all sorts flocking thither from the neighbouring tribes, and at the time we are speaking of the fear of raids had driven almost everyone off the land to the shelter of its walls. On Hannibal's approach this large and mixed population, emboldened by the report of the brave defence of the other trading-post near Placentia, flew to arms and marched out to meet him. Their long straggling line encountered his troops on the road – there was no attempt to form into battle order; they were no better than an undisciplined mob, while their antagonists were trained soldiers under an experienced commander, each enjoying the confidence of the other. They were easily routed – all 35,000 of them – though Hannibal's force was a mere handful.

Next day the fortress surrendered and was taken over by a Carthaginian garrison. All were ordered to lay down their arms, and as soon as the order was obeyed the signal was given to the victors to plunder the place as if it had been a city captured by assault. Of all the horrors which in circumstances of this sort historians like to record, not one was omitted: those unhappy people were the victims of every form of lust, cruelty, and inhuman beastliness. Such, then, were the activities of Hannibal during the winter.

1. BOCCACCIO · *Mrs Rosie and the Priest*
2. GERARD MANLEY HOPKINS · *As kingfishers catch fire*
3. *The Saga of Gunnlaug Serpent-tongue*
4. THOMAS DE QUINCEY · *On Murder Considered as One of the Fine Arts*
5. FRIEDRICH NIETZSCHE · *Aphorisms on Love and Hate*
6. JOHN RUSKIN · *Traffic*
7. PU SONGLING · *Wailing Ghosts*
8. JONATHAN SWIFT · *A Modest Proposal*
9. *Three Tang Dynasty Poets*
10. WALT WHITMAN · *On the Beach at Night Alone*
11. KENKŌ · *A Cup of Sake Beneath the Cherry Trees*
12. BALTASAR GRACIÁN · *How to Use Your Enemies*
13. JOHN KEATS · *The Eve of St Agnes*
14. THOMAS HARDY · *Woman much missed*
15. GUY DE MAUPASSANT · *Femme Fatale*
16. MARCO POLO · *Travels in the Land of Serpents and Pearls*
17. SUETONIUS · *Caligula*
18. APOLLONIUS OF RHODES · *Jason and Medea*
19. ROBERT LOUIS STEVENSON · *Olalla*
20. KARL MARX AND FRIEDRICH ENGELS · *The Communist Manifesto*
21. PETRONIUS · *Trimalchio's Feast*
22. JOHANN PETER HEBEL · *How a Ghastly Story Was Brought to Light by a Common or Garden Butcher's Dog*
23. HANS CHRISTIAN ANDERSEN · *The Tinder Box*
24. RUDYARD KIPLING · *The Gate of the Hundred Sorrows*
25. DANTE · *Circles of Hell*
26. HENRY MAYHEW · *Of Street Piemen*
27. HAFEZ · *The nightingales are drunk*
28. GEOFFREY CHAUCER · *The Wife of Bath*
29. MICHEL DE MONTAIGNE · *How We Weep and Laugh at the Same Thing*
30. THOMAS NASHE · *The Terrors of the Night*
31. EDGAR ALLAN POE · *The Tell-Tale Heart*
32. MARY KINGSLEY · *A Hippo Banquet*
33. JANE AUSTEN · *The Beautifull Cassandra*
34. ANTON CHEKHOV · *Gooseberries*
35. SAMUEL TAYLOR COLERIDGE · *Well, they are gone, and here must I remain*
36. JOHANN WOLFGANG VON GOETHE · *Sketchy, Doubtful, Incomplete Jottings*
37. CHARLES DICKENS · *The Great Winglebury Duel*
38. HERMAN MELVILLE · *The Maldive Shark*
39. ELIZABETH GASKELL · *The Old Nurse's Story*
40. NIKOLAY LESKOV · *The Steel Flea*

41. HONORÉ DE BALZAC · *The Atheist's Mass*
42. CHARLOTTE PERKINS GILMAN · *The Yellow Wall-Paper*
43. C. P. CAVAFY · *Remember, Body . . .*
44. FYODOR DOSTOEVSKY · *The Meek One*
45. GUSTAVE FLAUBERT · *A Simple Heart*
46. NIKOLAI GOGOL · *The Nose*
47. SAMUEL PEPYS · *The Great Fire of London*
48. EDITH WHARTON · *The Reckoning*
49. HENRY JAMES · *The Figure in the Carpet*
50. WILFRED OWEN · *Anthem For Doomed Youth*
51. WOLFGANG AMADEUS MOZART · *My Dearest Father*
52. PLATO · *Socrates' Defence*
53. CHRISTINA ROSSETTI · *Goblin Market*
54. *Sindbad the Sailor*
55. SOPHOCLES · *Antigone*
56. RYŪNOSUKE AKUTAGAWA · *The Life of a Stupid Man*
57. LEO TOLSTOY · *How Much Land Does A Man Need?*
58. GIORGIO VASARI · *Leonardo da Vinci*
59. OSCAR WILDE · *Lord Arthur Savile's Crime*
60. SHEN FU · *The Old Man of the Moon*
61. AESOP · *The Dolphins, the Whales and the Gudgeon*
62. MATSUO BASHŌ · *Lips too Chilled*
63. EMILY BRONTË · *The Night is Darkening Round Me*
64. JOSEPH CONRAD · *To-morrow*
65. RICHARD HAKLUYT · *The Voyage of Sir Francis Drake Around the Whole Globe*
66. KATE CHOPIN · *A Pair of Silk Stockings*
67. CHARLES DARWIN · *It was snowing butterflies*
68. BROTHERS GRIMM · *The Robber Bridegroom*
69. CATULLUS · *I Hate and I Love*
70. HOMER · *Circe and the Cyclops*
71. D. H. LAWRENCE · *Il Duro*
72. KATHERINE MANSFIELD · *Miss Brill*
73. OVID · *The Fall of Icarus*
74. SAPPHO · *Come Close*
75. IVAN TURGENEV · *Kasyan from the Beautiful Lands*
76. VIRGIL · *O Cruel Alexis*
77. H. G. WELLS · *A Slip under the Microscope*
78. HERODOTUS · *The Madness of Cambyses*
79. *Speaking of Siva*
80. *The Dhammapada*

81. JANE AUSTEN · *Lady Susan*
82. JEAN-JACQUES ROSSEAU · *The Body Politic*
83. JEAN DE LA FONTAINE · *The World is Full of Foolish Men*
84. H. G. WELLS · *The Sea Raiders*
85. LIVY · *Hannibal*
86. CHARLES DICKENS · *To Be Read at Dusk*
87. LEO TOLSTOY · *The Death of Ivan Ilyich*
88. MARK TWAIN · *The Stolen White Elephant*
89. WILLIAM BLAKE · *Tyger, Tyger*
90. SHERIDAN LE FANU · *Green Tea*
91. *The Yellow Book*
92. OLAUDAH EQUIANO · *Kidnapped*
93. EDGAR ALLAN POE · *A Modern Detective*
94. *The Suffragettes*
95. MARGERY KEMPE · *How To Be a Medieval Woman*
96. JOSEPH CONRAD · *Typhoon*
97. GIACOMO CASANOVA · *The Nun of Murano*
98. W. B. YEATS · *A terrible beauty is born*
99. THOMAS HARDY · *The Withered Arm*
100. EDWARD LEAR · *Nonsense*
101. ARISTOPHANES · *The Frogs*
102. FRIEDRICH NIETZSCHE · *Why I Am so Clever*
103. RAINER MARIA RILKE · *Letters to a Young Poet*
104. LEONID ANDREYEV · *Seven Hanged*
105. APHRA BEHN · *Oroonoko*
106. LEWIS CARROLL · *O frabjous day!*
107. JOHN GAY · *Trivia: or, the Art of Walking the Streets of London*
108. E. T. A. HOFFMANN · *The Sandman*
109. DANTE · *Love that moves the sun and other stars*
110. ALEXANDER PUSHKIN · *The Queen of Spades*
111. ANTON CHEKHOV · *A Nervous Breakdown*
112. KAKUZO OKAKURA · *The Book of Tea*
113. WILLIAM SHAKESPEARE · *Is this a dagger which I see before me?*
114. EMILY DICKINSON · *My life had stood a loaded gun*
115. LONGUS · *Daphnis and Chloe*
116. MARY SHELLEY · *Matilda*
117. GEORGE ELIOT · *The Lifted Veil*
118. FYODOR DOSTOYEVSKY · *White Nights*
119. OSCAR WILDE · *Only Dull People Are Brilliant at Breakfast*
120. VIRGINIA WOOLF · *Flush*
121. ARTHUR CONAN DOYLE · *Lot No. 249*

122. *The Rule of Benedict*
123. WASHINGTON IRVING · *Rip Van Winkle*
124. *Anecdotes of the Cynics*
125. VICTOR HUGO · *Waterloo*
126. CHARLOTTE BRONTË · *Stancliffe's Hotel*

‘We have nothing left in the world but what we can win with our swords.’

TITUS LIVY

Born 59 BC, Padua, Italy

Died AD 17, Rome, Italy

Livy's *History of Rome* consisted of 142 books of which 35 survive. This excerpt is taken from *The War with Hannibal* translated by Aubrey de Sélincourt, Penguin Classics, 1965.

LIVY IN PENGUIN CLASSICS

Rome and the Mediterranean

The War with Hannibal

Rome and Italy

The Early History of Rome